'Mud Stress Management'

21 Simple Hand Gestures for a Stress-Free Life

Advait

Disclaimer and FTC Notice

Advait

Contents

Mudras for Stress Management

Advait

What are Mudras?

According to the Vedic culture of ancient India, our entire world is made of 'the five elements' called as *The Panch-Maha-Bhuta's*. The five elements being **Earth**, **Water**, **Fire**, **Wind** and **Space/Vacuum**. They are also called the earth element, water element, fire element, wind element and space element.

These five elements constitute the human body – the nutrients from the soil (earth) are absorbed by the plants which we consume (thus we survive on the earth element), the blood flowing through own veins represents the water element, the body heat represents the fire element, the oxygen we inhale and the carbon dioxide we exhale represents the wind element and the sinuses we have in our nose and skull represent the space element.

As long as these five elements in our body are balanced and maintain appropriate levels we remain healthy. An imbalance of these elements in the human body leads to a deteriorated health and diseases.

Now understand this, the command and control center of all these five elements lies in our fingers. So literally, our health lies at our fingertips.

The Mudra healing method that I am going to teach you depends on our fingers.

To understand this, we should first know the finger-element relationship:

Thumb – Fire element.

Index finger – Wind element.

Middle finger – Space/Vacuum element.

Third finger – Earth element.

Small finger – Water element.

This image will give you a better understanding of the concept:

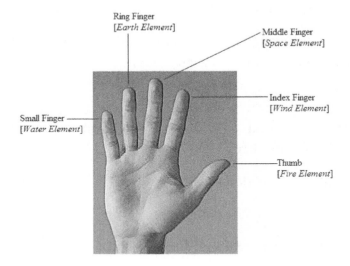

Ring Finger
[*Earth Element*]

Middle Finger
[*Space Element*]

Index Finger
[*Wind Element*]

Small Finger
[*Water Element*]

Thumb
[*Fire Element*]

When the fingers are brought together in a specific pattern and are touched to each other, or slightly pressed against each other, the formation is called as a *'Mudra'*.

When the five fingers are touched and pressed in a peculiar way to form a Mudra, it affects the levels of the five elements in our body, thus balancing those elements and inducing good health.

P.S. The Mudra Healing Methods aren't just theory or wordplay; these are healing methods

Mudras for Stress Management

from the ancient Indian Vedic culture, proven and tested over ages.

Attention!!

Read this before you read any further

For the better understanding of the reader, detail images have been provided for every mudra along with the method to perform it.

Most of the Mudras given in this book are to be performed using both your hands, but the Mudras whose images show only one hand performing the Mudra, are to be performed simultaneously on both your hands for the Mudras to have the maximum effect.

How to Use these Mudras?

All the Mudras mentioned in this book are Stress Reduction and Management Mudras which train you to remain Stress-Free and in Control in any kind of difficult situation and contribute towards a relaxed mind and help the practitioner maintain a calm composure all the time.

The Mudras in this book when performed regularly induce a special sense of peace and serenity in the practitioner.

These Mudras must be performed at a quiet place, sitting alone, preferably during meditation for maximum effect.

But, at times you would need to perform these Mudras when you feel stressed and since you would not be able to meditate while performing these Mudras, at least try and concentrate on your breathing and feel a calmness spreading all around you while you are performing these Mudras.

Also, understand that it is NOT a hard and fast rule that you should perform all these 21 Mudras back to back in one session.

Advait

Take your time, and perform these Mudras at your own pace and convenience.

The beauty of Mudra Health and Healing Techniques is that Mudras can be performed at any time and place: while stuck in traffic, at the office, watching TV, or whenever you have to twiddle your thumbs waiting for something or someone.

So, please don't come up with any excuses to avoid them, Mudras are as Easy and Effortless as Stress Management can get.

Mudra #1

Samputamudra / Mudra of Bud

Method:

It's a modified form of the 'Prayer Mudra'.

This Mudra is to be performed in a seated position.

Be seated comfortably in an upright posture and concentrate on your breathing to relax.

Advait

Touch the tip of the fingers of your right hand with the tip of the fingers of your left hand as shown in the image.

Make hollow space between both the palms as if you are holding a small bird.

Now, take this formation in front of your eyes, and look through the hollow space and concentrate on your breathing for a couple of minutes, then hold this Mudra in front of your Heart.

Duration:

This Mudra should be performed for at least 5 minutes and can be performed for 30 minutes at a stretch.

This Mudra should be performed twice a day, once in the morning and once in the evening for best results.

Mudra #2

Hridaymudra / Mudra of Heart

Method:

This Mudra is to be performed in a seated position.

Be seated comfortably in an upright posture and concentrate on your breathing to relax.

Try to touch the base of the Index finger with the tip of the same Index finger.

Advait

Now, roll this bent Index finger forward in such a way that the first knuckle of the Index finger touches the base of the Thumb (Refer the image).

Now join the tips of the Thumb, Middle and Ring fingers together and press slightly.

Keep the Little finger outstretched.

This Mudra is to be performed on both your palms simultaneously and then rest this Mudras on your thighs.

Duration:

This Mudra should be performed for at least 5 minutes and can be performed for 40 minutes at a stretch.

This Mudra should be performed twice a day, once in the morning and once in the evening for best results.

Mudra #3

Padmamudra / Mudra of Lotus

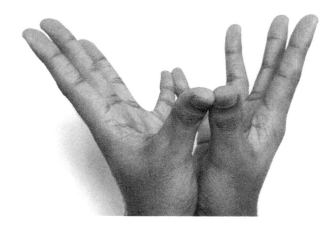

Method:

This Mudra is to be performed in a seated position.

Be seated comfortably in an upright posture and concentrate on your breathing to relax.

Touch the Thumb and Little finger of the left hand to the Thumb and Little finger of the right hand.

Join the base of both the palms together.

Advait

Stretch all the other fingers outwards and keep them straight.

Refer the image above.

This Mudra should be held in front of your chest.

Duration:

This Mudra should be performed for at least 5 minutes and can be performed for 40 minutes at a stretch.

This Mudra should be performed twice a day, once in the morning and once in the evening for best results.

Mudra #4

Tritiiya Kurmamudra / Mudra of Tortoise III

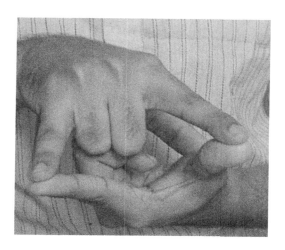

Method:

This Mudra is to be performed in a seated position.

Be seated comfortably in an upright posture and concentrate on your breathing to relax.

Advait

Raise your palms to chest height, with the left palm facing upwards while the right palm is facing downwards.

Curl down the Middle, Ring and Little fingers of the left hand to form a partial fist, while keeping the Index finger and Thumb extended.

Curl down the Middle and ring fingers of the right hand to form a partial fist, while keeping the Index finger, Little finger and the Thumb extended.

Now, keep the right palm over the left palm.

Then,

Touch the tip of the right Index finger to the tip of the left thumb.

Touch the tip of the right Little finger to the tip of the left Index finger.

Touch the tip of the right Thumb to the base of the left Thumb near the wrist.

After forming this Mudra, hold this Mudra in front of your Solar Plexus (just below your sternum)

Duration:

Mudras for Stress Management

This Mudra should be performed for at least 5 minutes and can be performed for 40 minutes at a stretch.

This Mudra should be performed twice a day, once in the morning and once in the evening for best results.

Mudra #5

Kaaleshwarmudra / Mudra of God of Time

Method:

This Mudra has to be performed in a seated position.

Be seated comfortably in an upright posture and concentrate on your breathing to relax.

Mudras for Stress Management

Touch the tip of the middle finger of your left hand with the tip of the middle finger of your right hand.

Touch the tip of the thumb of your left hand with the tip of the thumb of your right hand.

Keep the middle fingers and thumbs stretched and straight.

Bend the other fingers and let them touch each other at the joints, as shown in the image.

Hold this Mudra in front of your chest.

Duration:

This Mudra should be performed for at least 5 minutes and can be performed for 40 minutes at a stretch.

This Mudra should be performed twice a day, once in the morning and once in the evening for best results.

Advait

Mudra #6

Suryamudra / Mudra of Sun

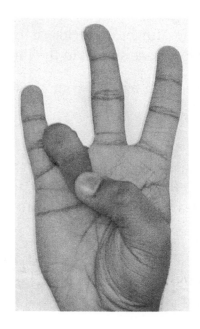

Method:

This Mudra can be performed while being seated, in a standing position or lying in bed.

Ideally, perform this Mudra in a seating position with your spine kept straight and upright.

Mudras for Stress Management

Concentrate on your breathing to relax and feel comfortable.

Place your hands on your thighs with your palms facing upwards.

Touch the nail of the Ring finger with the tip of your Thumb and press slightly.

Perform this Mudra for 30 minutes, on an empty stomach, first thing in the morning.

Duration:

This Mudra should be performed for at least 15 minutes and can be performed for 40 minutes at a stretch.

This Mudra should be performed twice a day, once in the morning and once in the evening for best results.

Mudra #7

Chakramudra / Mudra of Wheel

Method:

This Mudra is to be performed in a seated position.

Be seated comfortably in an upright posture and concentrate on your breathing to relax.

Mudras for Stress Management

Interlace your fingers together as shown in the image.

Extend both your Ring fingers upwards, then touch the tips of these two fingers and press slightly.

This Mudra is to be held in front of your navel.

Duration:

This Mudra should be performed for at least 5 minutes and can be performed for 40 minutes at a stretch.

This Mudra should be performed twice a day, once in the morning and once in the evening for best results.

Mudra #8

Tritiiya Varahamudra / Mudra of Hog III

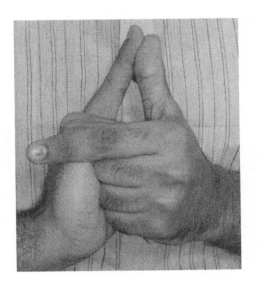

Method:

This Mudra is to be performed in a seated position.

Be seated comfortably in an upright posture and concentrate on your breathing to relax.

Mudras for Stress Management

Hold your left hand in front of your chest, palm facing you.

Curl the Middle, Ring and Little finger of the left hand inwards.

The Index finger should be pointing towards right and the Thumb should be extended upwards.

Now, clasp the curled fingers of the left hand with the fingers of the right hand.

Then, touch the tip of the Thumb of your left hand with the tip of the Index finger of your right hand.

Touch the tip of your right Thumb to the base of the left Thumb.

The Left Index finger should be resting outside the right Little finger.

Duration:

This Mudra should be performed for at least 5 minutes and can be performed for 45 minutes at a stretch.

This Mudra should be performed twice a day, once in the morning and once in the evening for best results.

Advait

Mudra #9

Hamsimudra / Mudra of Spirit Contained

Method:

This Mudra can be performed while being seated, in a standing position or lying in bed.

Concentrate on your breathing to relax and feel comfortable.

Mudras for Stress Management

Join the tips of your Middle finger, Ring finger, Little finger and Thumb together and press slightly.

Keep the Index finger extended outwards.

Duration:

No specific duration, perform as long as you wish, or, as long as it takes to achieve the desired effect.

Best results are obtained when performed for 15 minutes at a stretch.

Advait

Mudra #10

Phupphusmochanmudra / Mudra for Freeing lungs

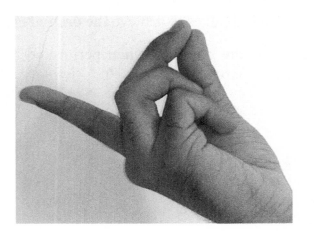

Method:

This Mudra can be performed while being seated, in a standing position or lying in bed.

Concentrate on your breathing to relax and feel comfortable.

Touch the tip of your Little finger to the base of the Thumb.

Mudras for Stress Management

Touch the tip of your Ring finger to the Middle of the Thumb.

Touch the tip of your Middle finger to the tip of the Thumb.

Keep the Index finger extended outwards. (Refer the image)

After performing the Mudra on both your hands, raise the Mudras to shoulder height and turn the palms away from you.

Relax your neck and shoulders.

Keep taking deep breaths while concentrating on your breathing and feel your chest and lungs opening up and drinking in the life energy.

Duration:

No specific duration, perform as long as you wish, or, as long as it takes to achieve the desired effect.

Best results are obtained when performed for 5 to 10 minutes at a stretch.

Advait

Mudra #11

Vyaapak Anjalimudra / Mudra of Offering

Method:

This Mudra is to be performed in a seated position.

Be seated comfortably in an upright posture and concentrate on your breathing to relax.

Now, with your palms facing upwards, curve the hands slightly, like forming a bowl and join the outer edges of your Little fingers. (Refer the image)

Once formed, hold this Mudra in front of your heart like you are making an offering.

Duration:

This Mudra should be performed for at least 5 minutes and can be performed for 45 minutes at a stretch.

This Mudra should be performed twice a day, once in the morning and once in the evening for best results.

Mudra #12

Mudgaramudra / Mudra of Club

Method:

This Mudra is to be performed in a seated position.

Be seated comfortably in an upright posture and concentrate on your breathing to relax.

Mudras for Stress Management

Form a fist with your right hand and rest the right elbow on the left palm.

(Refer the image)

Relax the shoulders and breathe comfortably.

Duration:

This Mudra should be performed for at least 5 minutes and can be performed for 30 minutes at a stretch.

This Mudra should be performed twice a day, once in the morning and once in the evening for best results.

Mudra #13

Chinmudra / Mudra of Consciousness

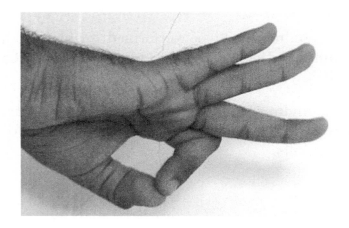

Method:

This Mudra is to be performed in a seated position.

Be seated comfortably in an upright posture and concentrate on your breathing to relax.

Lightly join the tip of the Index finger with the tip of the Thumb, while keeping all the other fingers relaxed and extended.

Mudras for Stress Management

Once the Mudra is formed, place the Mudra on your knees with your palms facing down.

Duration:

This Mudra should be performed for at least 5 minutes and can be performed for 45 minutes at a stretch.

This Mudra should be performed twice a day, once in the morning and once in the evening for best results.

Mudra #14

Pratham Uttarbodhimudra / Mudra of Supreme Awakening I

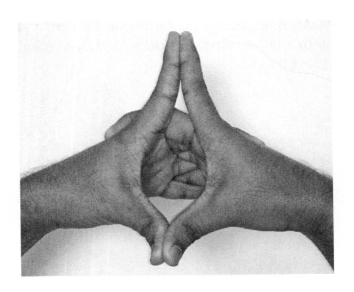

Method:

This Mudra can be performed while being seated, in a standing position or lying in bed.

Concentrate on your breathing to relax and feel comfortable.

Mudras for Stress Management

Interlace the fingers of both the hands together.

Now join the tips of the Index finger and the Thumbs together as shown in the image and extend the Index fingers as upwards as possible, simultaneously extending the Thumbs downwards.

(Refer the image for clarity.)

Duration:

This Mudra should be performed for at least 5 minutes and can be performed for 40 minutes at a stretch.

This Mudra should be performed twice a day, once in the morning and once in the evening for best results.

Mudra #15

Dwitiiya Uttarbodhimudra / Mudra of Supreme Awakening II

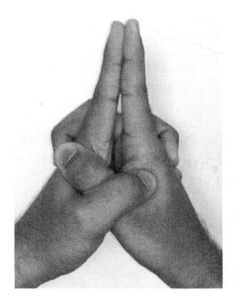

Method:

This Mudra is to be performed in a seated position.

Be seated comfortably in an upright posture and concentrate on your breathing to relax.

Mudras for Stress Management

Clasp your hands together, and interlace the fingers of both the hands together.

Now join the tips of the Index finger as shown in the image and extend the Index fingers as upwards as possible,

Then cross-over the left Thumb on the right Thumb.

(Refer the image)

Duration:

This Mudra should be performed for at least 5 minutes and can be performed for 40 minutes at a stretch.

This Mudra should be performed twice a day, once in the morning and once in the evening for best results.

Mudra #16

Sinhkraantamudra / Mudra of Lion's Paw

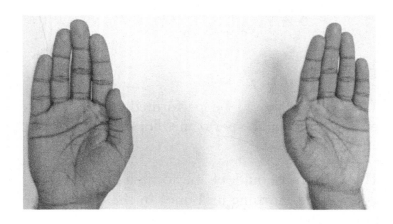

Method:

This Mudra is to be performed in a seated position.

Be seated comfortably in an upright posture and concentrate on your breathing to relax.

Lift your palms at shoulder height with the palms facing away from you.

Mudras for Stress Management

Extend all the fingers upwards, and touching each other at the sides.

(Refer the image)

Hold this Mudra at the shoulder level.

Duration:

This Mudra should be performed for at least 5 minutes and can be performed for 30 minutes at a stretch.

This Mudra should be performed twice a day, once in the morning and once in the evening for best results.

Mudra #17

Lingamudra / Mudra of Divine Masculine

Method:

This Mudra is to be performed in a seated position.

Be seated comfortably in an upright posture and concentrate on your breathing to relax.

Mudras for Stress Management

Clasp the fingers of both of your hands as shown in the image.

Keep the Thumb of your left hand straight and erect.

This Mudra is to be held in front of your abdomen.

(This Mudra is about bringing all the five elements together, with the fire element ruling them all.)

Duration:

It's a highly effective Mudra, yet a very strong one.

Perform this Mudra for not more than 5-7 minutes at a time.

This Mudra creates a lot of heat in the body, so don't overdo it.

Mudra #18

Dnyaanamudra / Mudra of Wisdom

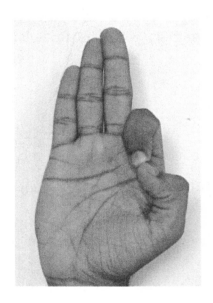

Method:

This Mudra is to be performed in a seated position.

Be seated comfortably in an upright posture and concentrate on your breathing to relax.

Mudras for Stress Management

Join the tips of your Index finger and Thumb together and press slightly.

Keep all the other fingers extended outwards as shown in the image.

After forming the Mudras on both the hands, rest the Mudras on your thighs, palms facing up.

Duration:

This Mudra should be performed for at least 5 minutes and can be performed for 20 minutes at a stretch.

This Mudra should be performed twice a day, once in the morning and once in the evening for best results.

Mudra #19

Sahastraarmudra / Mudra of Thousand Petals

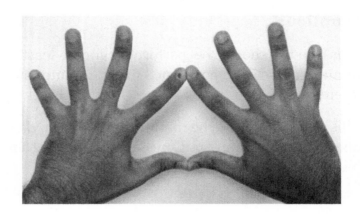

Method:

This Mudra can be performed while being seated or in a standing position.

Concentrate on your breathing to relax and feel comfortable.

Raise your hands at chest height, with your palms facing down.

Mudras for Stress Management

Now, join the tips of both the Index fingers together and press slightly.

Then, join the tips of both the Thumbs together forming a Triangle. (Refer the image)

Keep all the other fingers extended and outstretched.

Once you have formed this Mudra, raise the Mudra at a height of around 6 inches above your head.

And now visualize as if a shower of light and energy are entering the top of your head through the triangle formed in the Mudra.

Duration:

This Mudra should be performed for at least 5 minutes and can be performed for 20 minutes at a stretch.

This Mudra should be performed twice a day, once in the morning and once in the evening for best results.

Advait

Mudra #20

Garudamudra / Mudra of Eagle

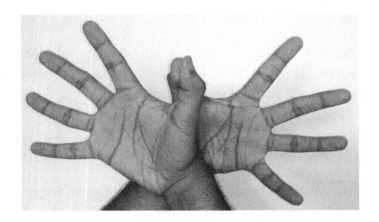

Method:

This Mudra can be performed while being seated, in a standing position or lying in bed.

Concentrate on your breathing to relax and feel comfortable.

Bring both your hands in front of your chest, palms facing the chest.

Mudras for Stress Management

Cross the hands with the right hand crossing over the left hand and interlock the Thumbs at the first padding. (Refer the image)

Keep all the other fingers extended and outstretched.

Create a firm pressure between the pads of the Thumb.

Duration:

This Mudra should be performed for at least 5 minutes and can be performed for 40 minutes at a stretch.

This Mudra should be performed twice a day, once in the morning and once in the evening for best results.

Mudra #21

Rudramudra / Mudra of Lord Shiva

Method:

This Mudra is to be performed in a seated position.

Be seated comfortably in an upright posture and concentrate on your breathing to relax.

Place your hands on your thighs with your palms facing upwards.

Mudras for Stress Management

Touch the tip of your Thumb with the tip of your Index finger and the tip of the Ring finger, press slightly.

Refer the image for more clarity.

Duration:

This Mudra should be performed for at least 5 minutes and can be performed for 40 minutes at a stretch.

If you are serious about losing weight then this Mudra should be performed at least 4 times a day.

Advait

Thank You

Thank you so much for reading my book. I hope you really liked it.

As you probably know, many people look at the reviews on Amazon before they decide to purchase a book.

If you liked the book, please take a minute to leave a review with your feedback.

60 seconds is all I'm asking for, and it would mean a lot to me.

Thank You so much.

All the best,

Advait

Other Books by Advait

Mudras for Awakening Chakras: 19 Simple Hand Gestures for Awakening & Balancing Your Chakras

http://www.amazon.com/dp/B00P82COAY

[#1 Bestseller in 'Yoga']

[#1 Bestseller in 'Chakras']

Advait

Mudras for Weight Loss: 21 Simple Hand
Gestures for Effortless Weight Loss

http://www.amazon.com/dp/B00P3ZPSEK

Mudras for Stress Management

Mudras for Spiritual Healing: 21 Simple Hand Gestures for Ultimate Spiritual Healing & Awakening

http://www.amazon.com/dp/B00PFYZLQO

Mudras for Sex: 25 Simple Hand Gestures for
Extreme Erotic Pleasure & Sexual Vitality

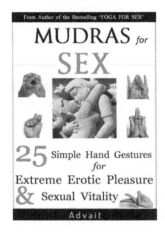

http://www.amazon.com/dp/B00OJR1DRY

Mudras for Stress Management

Mudras: 25 Ultimate Techniques for Self Healing

http://www.amazon.com/dp/B00MMPB5CI

Mudras of Anxiety: 25 Simple Hand Gestures for Curing Anxiety

http://www.amazon.com/dp/B00PF011IU

Mudras for Stress Management

Mudras for a Strong Heart: 21 Simple Hand Gestures for Preventing, Curing & Reversing Heart Disease

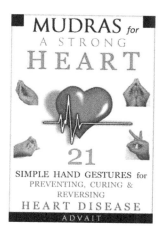

http://www.amazon.com/dp/B00PFRLGTM

Mudras for Curing Cancer: 21 Simple Hand
Gestures for Preventing & Curing Cancer

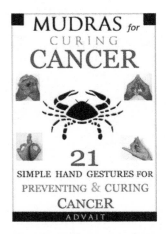

http://www.amazon.com/dp/B00PFO199M

Mudras for Stress Management

Mudras for Stress Management: 21 Simple Hand Gestures for a Stress Free Life

http://amazon.com/dp/B00PFTJ6OC

Mudras for Memory Improvement: 25 Simple
Hand Gestures for Ultimate Memory
Improvement

http://www.amazon.com/dp/B00PFSP8TK

Mudras for Stress Management

Made in the USA
Monee, IL
11 June 2023